'WESTERN' DIESELS in camera

LONDON
IAN ALLAN LTD

'WESTERN' DIESELS in camera

J. A. M. Vaughan

First published 1977

Reprinted 1978

ISBN 0 7110 0831 0

Published by Ian Allan Ltd, Shepperton, Surrey, and printed in the United Kingdom by Ian Allan Printing Ltd.

Introduction

Born towards the end of British main line steam, the 'Westerns' were to the majority of steam enthusiasts just another box on wheels — a diesel, impersonal and lacking the character and aesthetic attraction of the iron horse. Yet within a decade they commanded a following of a vast number of supporters, many of whom had almost ignored the 'Westerns' at the end of steam. The last two or three years in particular have seen the 'Westerns' enjoying a popularity which without any doubt has been the most fanatical since steam finished on British Rail's standard-gauge lines.

The reasons for this popularity are numerous. By deciding that locomotives with diesel-electric transmission would be the norm the decision-makers in the corridors of power inadvertently elevated the 'Westerns' (and to a lesser extent the 'Warships' and 'Hymeks') to the pedestal of the non-standard which has always attracted railway enthusiasts. The first withdrawal of the diesel-hydraulic locomotives reinforced this attraction.

The 'Westerns' in many ways perpetuated the autonomy of a pre-nationalisation regime. The cast name and number plates were in the finest Great Western Railway tradition, even though the material used was alloy and not brass. The cast number plates prevented the 'Westerns' being renumbered when designated Class 52 in the BR renumbering scheme. This made them unique in an era when management did not favour naming engines and all locomotive numbers were either painted or stencilled on to the paintwork. The names themselves were pompous, arrogant and superior, resisting any suggestion that they formed part of a national system.

From the embryo stage the 'Westerns' were to be distinctive in styling and typically (G)WR. They were built at Swindon and Crewe in the best tradition, but using modern techniques. They were certainly the most handsome diesel locomotives built for British Railways and liveries were varied in the early days. The two V12 high-speed Bristol Siddeley Maybach engines produced the most exciting sound, suggesting great power and fierce activity, especially when compared with the slow speed rumble of the majority of diesel electrics. This sound was recognised and recorded on a long playing record of 'Western' sounds.

The first withdrawals occurred during 1973 and by that time enthusiasts and photographers were making special pilgrimages to the familiar haunts of the 'Westerns' to record their last days on film, not suspecting that these fine locomotives would resist extinction for several years. In the latter years some of the 'Westerns' looked decidedly shabby, but still the cameras clicked. During their last summer of main-line service, 1976, hordes of enthusiasts were travelling behind 'Westerns' at every opportunity to increase their recorded mileage or just for enjoyment. This enthusiasm culminated in a spate of specials which were mostly over-subscribed.

'Westerns' were also known as Type 4 C-C, Class 4 diesel-hydraulics, Class 52s, 1000 class (by Cornish railwaymen), 'Wizzos' (by the mileage men) and 'Wezzies' (by the younger element of train-spotters). Many of the locomotives had their own nicknames in later years. As the number of engine withdrawals increased so did enthusiasm, which in railway circles seems to be a natural phenomenon. The selling prices of nameplates increased tenfold and rivalled even those fetched by the brass examples of their steam predecessors. All of these features consolidated the popularity of the 'Westerns'.

On a more personal note I must confess that I started to take a special interest in 'Westerns' during 1971, after the withdrawals of the 'Warships' had commenced. The attraction grew and by 1976 had become almost an obsession. From Paddington to Penzance, from Filton to Fishguard and from Birmingham to Brighton the class were sought, chased, travelled behind and photographed. My other interests of branch lines and steam traction adopted a minor role. Finally my efforts and those of many contributors resulted in the preparation of this volume, which I hope will have memorable associations for readers.

I have heard much discussion about 'Westerns' between colleagues, railwaymen and enthusiasts. Nobody could claim that in terms of overall design, availability or performance they were the greatest diesel locomotives ever built. In common with most new machinery they had their share of teething troubles, but by the mid-1960s they were giving sterling service. When fully extended they occasionally achieved a three-figure speed, even though their service speed was never higher than 90. On their day they were always a match for the Class 47s and in terms of initial acceleration they were infinitely superior. One other advantage afforded by virtue of their two engines was the ability to soldier along, and indeed put up quite a showing, on one engine.

Sadly in their last days one engine-running was a frequent occurrence, caused largely by neglect in maintenance coupled with high-mileage rosters. During the latter part of 1976 the number of 'Westerns' on shed could almost be determined by the density of the cloud of diesel exhaust fumes hovering overhead. They were worn out. The usual frantic scenes of farewell railtours occurred between October 1976 and February 1977, and I had the pleasure of organising four of them. The tours were heavily over-subscribed and I was amazed at the truly nationwide demand for tickets.

As with steam the 'Westerns' passed. They will hold a special place in the hearts of those who pursued them. Thankfully the preservation movement will ensure their place for posterity. Whilst the joyous sound of the 'Westerns' may not be heard again climbing up to Savernake with a train of holidaymakers, ascending the Fowey Valley with china clay or carrying hundreds of enthusiasts on some obscure line, they will undoubtedly be heard on one stretch of preserved track or another.

I would like to thank the following individuals and concerns for the help and assistance I have received in the research, compilation and presentation of this album: my publishers for the freedom allowed in the selection of material; fellow railway photographers and contributors; my wife for moral support; Janet Cole for secretarial services; Rodney Smith and John Frith for advice; BR Engineering Ltd; numerous railwaymen; and finally the author of the formal introduction Michael Sawyer the British Railways, WR, Locomotive Development Engineer.

John A. M. Vaughan

The Class 52 in Retrospect

BY M. G. SAWYER B.Sc. (Mech Eng), C.Eng., M.I. Mech. E.
Locomotive Development Engineer, British Railways, Western Region

The Beginning

When, in 1955, a decision was made by the then British Transport Commission to eliminate steam from British Railways, replacing it by electric and diesel traction, there was still sufficient autonomy in the Regions for each to design and sponsor its own choice of locomotives or multiple-unit trains, and to have them built either in their own Workshops or by private industry.

German industry, too, was reviving after the war, but the lack of electrical industry in that country at that time led firms such as Maybach, Voith and Krauss-Maffei to develop forms of traction conceived before the war, which reduced the electrical element to the minimum. Working in conjunction with the Deutches Bundesbahn, they saw that a high-speed engine running at around 1,500 rpm, combined with a hydro-dynamic drive, gave enormous possibilities to produce locomotives much lighter for their power than anything which could be produced with diesel-electric transmission.

So was born the V200 series of B-B locomotives of some 2,200hp, weighing only some 80tons — quite an achievement for the period. Following those, several developments came along with increasing engine power and hauling capacity. Amongst these was the ML 3000, a C-C locomotive which was to become the basic pattern for the D1000s. The then General Manager of the Western Region, Mr K. W. C. Grand and his Chief Mechanical Engineer, Mr R. A. Smeddle, also saw things rather along these lines. The Western Region design office and works had little experience of electric traction matters and the Region also saw possibilities of building high-powered locomotives with good adhesion and all-round haulage capacity, which could work fast and heavy trains into the West Country, in particular over the Royal Albert Bridge at Saltash, where their predecessors, the steam 'Kings', had not been allowed to go,

The first diesel-hydraulics to be built at Swindon were the D800 'Warships', each of which had two Maybach MD650 engines of 1,100hp driving a Maybach-Mekydro hydraulic transmission and thence four axles. These locomotives bore a very marked resemblance to the German V200 series and were, in fact, produced from drawings deriving directly from the Krauss-Maffei V200 design, although major alterations had to be made to bring the locomotives within the British loading gauge. The underframes were based upon two longitudinal tubes passing through, and welded to, cross platings and the bodies were built on a stressed skin principle; it was probably the first real application of the stressed skin principle to locomotives in Britain.

The Maybach-Mekydro transmission consisted of a torque converter driving a four-speed gear box. Gear changing took place at selected speeds, determined by a combination of vehicle speed and engine speed. This enabled the converter always to be operating near its most efficient point. When a gear change was initiated, the turbine wheel of the converter was withdrawn slightly, so putting 'on stream' a different set of blades incorporated in the same rotor, which gave a weak backward movement to the gear train. Since the primary gears of each pair were driven by ratchets, these disengaged under the reverse movement, enabling the drive to be transferred from one pair of gears to another. As soon as the actual physical part of the change was complete, the turbine wheel was then pushed back into place, once again allowing the full power of the engine to be passed through the transmission.

At the same time, locomotives were built by the North British Locomotive Company, using MAN 12-cylinder engines of 1,000hp. Most of these engines were built by NBL and the driving transmissions also, but the latter were to the design of and used some parts produced by Maybach's rival in the hydraulic transmission field — Voith of Heidenheim. Voith avoided the mechanical gear change, which they rightly saw as a feature likely to give rise to wear and unreliability. Instead, they used three separate torque converters, each with a slightly different characteristic and each driving the output shaft through a pair of gear wheels always in constant mesh. Gears were again selected on the basis of train speed, with an engine speed bias, but the actual change was carried out by emptying and filling each converter with hydraulic oil in turn.

The first North British Type 4 Locomotives had certain problems which caused them not to be perpetuated. They were the first to be scrapped when a decision was eventually made to run down the diesel-hydraulic fleet. However, the power equipment — MAN engine and Voith transmissionwere- incorporated in 33 locomotives of the Krauss-Maffei-based 'Warship' design, built this time by NBL.

Before passing on to the 'Westerns', we must not forget the 'Hymeks', built by Beyer Peacock with Maybach 16-cylinder engines using Mekydro transmissions. Such was the state of the diesel hydraulic art in 1959.

In the meantime, experience was being obtained with all these types of locomotives on different services. Evidence pointed at the time to the superiority of the Maybach engine over the MAN, in particular in its capacity to develop more power. The roller-bearing mounted crankshaft proved highly reliable, despite apprehension on some people's part. The British licensees of Maybach-Bristol-Siddeley, as it was at the time — had produced an ambitious works layout at their Anstey works which was turning out excellent workmanship. On the other hand, the MAN engine of the time had problems, mainly with pistons and with the exhaust system. There was little enthusiasm for the proposed uprated version, which was both larger and heavier than Maybach's equivalent. The 'Warship' locomotive body and bogie had been very satisfactory, give or take early problems with the pivotless centre arrangement and with cracked axles. The cabs were roomy and comfortable, the drivers liked them and the axle bearing radius arm links, instead of the then conventional sliding axlebox guides with manganese rubbing liners, were clearly a big step forward. Therefore, when the next batch of locomotives was being conceived, the choice fell upon a Krauss-Maffei type mechanical design using the Maybach engine, and the German ML3000 being taken as the starting point.

The Inception of the D1000s

Meanwhile other Regions of BR, in conjunction with other manufacturers, were developing the diesel-electric locomotive. Having tasted the capabilities of diesel power, the marketeers and operators were thirsting for better and better performance. So, after the first Type 4 Derby-Sulzers developing 2,300hp, the next batch was rated at 2,500hp and the one after that at 2,750hp, although some engine structural problems which developed in the early part of their life caused their ratings subsequently to be reduced to 2,580hp.

Likewise on the Western Region, there was a cry for more competitive schedules, especially to the West of England, where a three-and-a-half hour timing between London and Plymouth was envisaged for the two prestige trains of the day, the 'Cornish Riviera Limited' and the 'Golden Hind'. It was obvious that more powerful locomotives than the 'Warships' were going to be required and design work recommenced at Swindon.

By this time, Maybach were offering their 12 MD engine at a rating of 1350hp and both Voith and Maybach had further developed their transmissions to transmit the increased power. As far as the engine was concerned, the extra power came from increasing the fuel input, producing more air from basically the same turbo-blower and cooling the air with a charge inter-cooler before admitting it to the cylinders. In this way a larger weight of air (because cool air is heavier than hot air) could be available in the cylinder at the right time to burn the increased quantity of fuel. The penalty of this charge air inter-cooling is that the water which cools the air has in turn to be cooled and this means a bigger radiator. Also, because the transmission is now dealing with more power and because the heat produced in the transmission in the process of 'torque conversion' is proportional to the power, extra cooling capacity must be provided in the radiator to deal with it.

With the all-round increase in weight which resulted from the increased performance demanded of many of the components, the overall body weight was growing somewhat. At the same time, the extra power meant that extra tractive effort would be available through out the speed range from starting to 90mph; the question was how to obtain the best advantage from this. The weight per axle was already at its limit on the D800s and it was therefore natural to go to a C-C wheel arrangement, utilising six final drive units similar to those already used on the 'Warships' and the 'Hymeks'. This arrangement enabled the tractive effort to be achieved comfortably without increasing the ratio of tractive effort at wheel tread divided by the weight of each wheel on the track; this ratio is known as the available adhesion ratio and must be kept to within 30% if slipping is not to become a problem.

The question then arose as to how to get the power from the transmission to the six axles. Because of the geometry of the layout, it was no longer possible to continue the arrangement whereby each transmission drove two final gearboxes by cardan shafts connected to the two ends of the transmission output shaft. Instead, each transmission was to drive an intermediate gearbox mounted on the bogie frame, whence the drive was then distributed to the axles.

It was the deliberations at this stage of the design work which finally decided the Western Region to opt for the Voith transmission rather than the Mekydro. The Mekydro box just could not fit into any arrangement compatible with the British loading gauge.

The coupling together of the axles in threes through cardan shafts prevented the ill-effects of weight transfer. This gave the D1000s their excellent-road holding characteristic, which has done the Western Region so proud on heavy trains on the West Country banks. Weight transfer, for the uninitiated, is the tendency for the leading end of the locomotive or individual bogie to rise in the air and the trailing end to sit down on its haunches, so to speak, when pulling hard. On an individual axle drive such as we have with diesel-electric locomotives, this can cause the leading pair of wheels to spin. When all the wheels are coupled together, this spinning of individual wheels cannot occur, even if there is no weight on the axle.

Building

With the design completed the next question was how many should be built and where. The plan was to cover most of the London to Bristol, Birmingham and Swansea passenger services, as well as the Paddington to West of England services, the latter normally as far as Plymouth, although some trains were planned for through working to Penzance. Locomotive changing at Plymouth enabled a less powerful locomotive, such as a 'Warship', to work a train lightened by two or three coaches through Cornwall, where the line speed was not so high and haulage did not demand so much power.

As a first go, 74 locomotives were authorised, although at that stage it was envisaged that many more would eventually be built. The policy at that time was to eliminate steam by 1964 and use had to be made of all the workshop capacity available in order to produce sufficient locomotives in time.

As the 1000 Class was designed at Swindon, Swindon was naturally the first choice as a building centre. However, their building rate was limited and other resources had to be brought in. The Railway Workshops had by that time, been hived off from the Regions and put under one separate management. Thus Crewe came into the picture as the obvious choice for an alternative building works, since it had not so far been fully utilised in the dieselisation programme. Crewe had, in fact, just started on a programme of building some Type 2 Derby-Sulzer (later designated Class 24 and 25) locomotives, but their diesel building capacity had not yet been fully exploited. In the event, Swindon laid down the first frame and produced the first locomotive, D1000 *Western Enterprise*, which entered traffic on 20 December 1961. This was followed by Nos D1001 to D1029. The first Crewe locomotive, D1035 *Western Yeoman*, was delivered to the Western Region on 27 July 1962 followed by locomotives Nos D1036 to D1073 and D1030 to D1034. Erections of the latter group had originally been planned for Swindon.

The first locomotives entered traffic in a variety of experimental liveries — D1000 in Desert Sand, D1001 in LMSR maroon, D1002 to 1005 in Brunswick green and D1015 in golden ochre, a precise match with Stroudley's *Gladstone*. The first Crewe locomotives were painted in Brunswick green but LMS maroon was adopted after D1038. Eventually all locomotives except D1036 were repainted in maroon until, under British Railways' corporate identity scheme, all the locomotives were gradually repainted in Rail Blue with yellow fronts. This livery was maintained to the end.

In Service

The 74 locomotives were allocated to depots at Bristol Bath Road, Cardiff Canton, Swansea Landore and Plymouth Laira. They gained great popularity with train crews because of their good ride, comfortable cab, smooth take-up of power without slip, almost imperceptible gear changes, the power available for hauling heavy freight trains and the high speeds sustainable on passenger trains. Perhaps the greatest asset of the locomotives was the virtually duplicated power equipment; if one engine or transmission failed there was usually the other one to get the train home. This was frequently done, sometimes only losing some 15min between Taunton and London, compared with often 50min delay when a single-engined diesel electric failed and had to be replaced. The confidence placed in the 1000s was exemplified in the choice of the locomotives for nearly all royal and special occasions, to within a year or so of their final withdrawal from service.

Against this, there were technical problems. Initially, failures of final drives nearly grounded the fleet. This problem, however, was simple to overcome. Then there were failures of bearings in the transmissions. Complex investigations were carried out involving vibration analysis and it was found that oscillations produced by the rocking of the final drives were causing vibrations harmful to the bearings in the transmissions. Extensive modifications to the torque arm suspension of the final drives were contemplated, but eventually it was decided as a first measure to replace some of the bearings in the output shaft of the transmissions with an arrangement rather more robust. This modification cured the problem, so that the more extensive alterations on the gearbox suspension were never needed.

Then there were problems with cracking of the bogie frames. Various strengthening modifications were carried out under the auspices of the now BRB-controlled design section at Swindon. Although the cracking was contained, some radical re-design was clearly required. By that time, however, there were already doubts about the future of the locomotives and the re-design was never pursued.

Probably the most serious problem to befall the locomotives was the cracking of cylinder heads. The cylinder head was of a very ambitious design, containing six valves, three inlet and three exhaust, surrounding the central injector and pre-combustion chamber. The whole design was really too critical and, despite strengthening, the cracking, especially around the pre-combustion chamber, became very prevalent.

Unfortunately the cracking of one cylinder head often led to high pressure gases entering the cooling system, giving rise to lack of cooling and consequent hot spots in other cylinders. This would set off a chain reaction, cracking sometimes six other heads before any trouble was suspected. In conjunction with Maybach, an elaborate venting system was designed, aimed at bleeding off any air in the system before it could cause damage. Later, this venting system was developed to include a centrifugal 'bubble separator' placed in the main water outlet from the engine. This sent the coolant swirling in the pipe. A small pipe inserted into the main pipe at the eye of the vortex bled off any air or gas which had entered the system through cracks and so completely prevented re-circulation. These combined efforts virtually eliminated the epidemic head cracking, but sporadic cracking continued to the end of the life of the locomotives.

From the outset, there had been one or two cases of cracking turbo-blower gas inlet casings. Suddenly these failures became more numerous and reached serious proportions. Investigations showed that the stress in the casing was far too high, but despite deep investigation and tightening of overhaul and testing procedures, the cracking was never cured and neither was a satisfactory reason found for the sudden increase in failures in 1969. The puzzle dies with the locomotives.

One of the philosophies behind the Western Region diesel-hydraulics was that they should only go to Works for repair at extended intervals — 4 to 5 years in the case of the 1000s. Engines, though, required a light overhaul at 6,000 hours or after approximately 18 months operation. The lightness and compactness of the engines and transmissions was such that these components could be lifted out of locomotives in the depot and replaced by overhauled units, all within the space of less than a day. Thus two engine changes would normally be carried out at the depot between works visits. Facilities were also provided at several depots on the region to jack locomotives for bogies to be run out and replaced by works-reconditioned units.

A service of special wagons, converted Weltrols and horseboxes, was instituted to take these major components to and from Works. This saved many locomotive months in works and enabled maximum life to be obtained from components, since the changes did not have to be carried out coincidentally with other work. Indeed, this philosophy has lately had its spin-off in the field of the diesel-electric locomotive. The depot facilities, primarily provided for the diesel-hydraulic locomotives, have had their uses for the diesel-electric fleet and have spread a new way of thinking about depot economics throughout British Railways. For instance, depot jacking equipment provided initially for the diesel-hydraulics has enabled changes of bogies to be made on diesel-electric locomotives virtually overnight.

It is worth saying a word about re-numbering. When, in 1967, computers were first introduced seriously to British Railways, it was important to be able to refer to locomotives by a simple code. Previously we had referred to Types 1, 2, 3, 4 and 5, according to the horsepower range of the locomotive and we had then gone into a complicated description to identify the exact type we were discussing. The new type numbers classified locomotives in ascending order of power and the 1000 class, or 1XXX in the Western Region terminology of the time, became Class 52. Later, the numbering was taken to its logical conclusion by combining the class number and number within the class in one — for example, 47 149; but because of the impending withdrawal — coupled, perhaps with a little nostalgia and reluctance to removed the polished cast aluminium numbers this was not done with the Class 52s, so that a little of the original individuality of the class survived.

The Run Down

By 1963, dieselisation or electrification was almost complete and, with the new knowledge that even with the huge investment in motive power made over the previous five years, British Railways was far from paying its way, the new Chairman, Dr Beeching introduced his famous plan. The Board, once the plan had been accepted, quickly saw that a reduction in the locomotive fleet was inevitable.

A group at Marylebone began to formulate a National Traction Plan. It was already clear that the then Chief Engineer T&RS, at the Board favoured the diesel-electric locomotive over the diesel-hydraulic and in fact the Brush Sulzer Type 4 — later Class 47 — had already been recognised as the standard Type 4 Locomotive.

The diesel-hydraulic fleet had its problems, as can be seen. Much of it was thought in influential quarters to be endemic in the design conception. Later, as problems were resolved — but too late to save the hydraulics — this was seen not to be so. Nevertheless, statistics showed that these particular hydraulics were still much more expensive to run and maintain than the diesel-electrics and, it must be admitted by even the most devoted enthusiasts, the alterations required to make maintenance viable would have been so expensive that there could never have been a pay-off during the maximum expected life of the locomotives.

Out of this thinking came the decision to scrap the earlier diesel-hydraulics: first the MAN-engined locomotives, then the Maybach D800s, then the 'Hymeks', but leaving for a time the D1000s, although there was some to-ing and fro-ing of opinion about the future of these from the start. Finally, in 1970, the prediction of the National Traction Plan group having been proved correct so far and although a great deal of work had been done successfully to cure some of their problems, the decision was made to run down the D1000 Class. In order to achieve some economy in works costs, the overhaul rate was increased considerably. Thus the erecting shop and supporting facilities at Swindon could be freed quickly from the responsibility of dealing with the diesel-hydraulics and be turned over completely to other work. Otherwise, Swindon would have been left with a slowly reducing and increasingly uneconomical diesel-hydraulic locomotive commitment.

Following these last overhauls, the last span of life

began. At first there was a plan to overhaul and repair engines, transmissions, bogies and all ancillary apparatus at Swindon on a reduced scale. The policy for returning parts to Works for overhaul, instead of being based on the principle of preventative maintenance, became one of repair, not exactly on failure but when there were signs of distress. Such signs as passing too much oil into the exhaust, incorrect gear change in transmissions and other symptoms already known to be indicative of the need of repair became the criteria for overhaul. In fact, the sort of principles adopted by a motor fleet operator were applied by the Western Region to the Class 52. This policy worked well. In fact, surprisingly long lives between overhauls were obtained with parts, which threw some doubt on the intervals between repairs on which the Region had been operating. Of course, with a fleet having a much higher potential life one could not adopt such procedures, as it would inevitably produce expensive failures of a kind which, in a run-down situation, did not have to be put right.

The first stage of the run-down was to withdraw the locomotives from the South Wales workings, concentrating them on Bristol Bath Road and Laira. The South Wales and some of the Bristol services were being taken over by Class 47 locomotives, converted so as to be able to supply electric power to air-conditioned coaches.

At the same time, Class 50s were beginning to arrive from the London Midland Region and were taking over more of the duties of the Class 52s on the London to Bristol and West of England routes. With the arrival of the Class 50s the run-down was accelerated by the reduction of the number of component repairs undertaken at Swindon. Thus, when an engine ceased to be serviceable, the locomotive was put out of service and cannibalised to provide spares — including the good engine — for other locomotives.

Major power equipment parts were not the only critical factors in condemning locomotives. Such things as general aging of wiring — not surprising after a life of some 14 years — tended to make repairs uneconomic, as did the occasional tiff with another locomotive in the yard. This often caused minor structural damage behind the buffer beam, and would in former times have been repaired by cutting out the damaged section and welding in a prefabricated replacement. So, gradually, the fleet was worked out. By the end of 1975, 35 locomotives were left in service. Officially they were diagrammed to freight services only, on the ground that with a slight degree of engine de-rating subtly introduced, and the lower speeds for freight work, the maximum amount of remaining life could be obtained from the locomotives.

It is to be noted that the locomotives throughout this trying period continued to defy all predictions as to possible run-down rates. In fact, with delays in the introduction of HST, combined with several items of new freight haulage business won somewhat unexpectedly from road competitors, the railway should be grateful for the tenacity of the Class 52s in the last dying years.

In October 1976, with the beginning of the introduction of HST, all further repairs of parts at Swindon were stopped and a quick run-down ensued. No locomotive was expected to survive after February 1977 save one, which is to be preserved for prosperity in York Museum, plus possibly one or two preserved privately.

Stepping Stones to the future

An era has passed, with regrets and nostalgia for some. But from the point of view of the railway engineer, it has been far from in vain. We have learned many lessons from the Class 52s. In some cases obviously, sometimes hardly recognisably, they have paved the way ahead. We have learned a lot about the high-speed engine: how to make it work and how to mount it so that it is both accessible for everyday maintenance and at the same time easily lifted out and replaced for overhaul; how to play the module game, with radiators in particular; how components can be made and included in the design so that people think in terms of taking them out and putting another one in when things go wrong, rather than repairing them somewhat awkwardly, in situ; and how to design a cab that drivers like and which Ministry officers approve. We have looked at small details such as warning lights for mechanical defects — red for danger and blue for 'all in order', so that the exact situation is clear and there is no query that it is just a bulb which has burned out. We know that it pays not to skimp on battery size; only very rarely have we had a case of a flat battery, despite lights left on overnight and all the hazards of trying to start engines that don't want to start. We have identified many things not to be frightened of should they reappear in the future — the roller bearing-mounted crankshaft, for instance; failures have been very rare. We know now how to design a reliable hydrostatic fan drive; many of the modifications incorporated in Class 52s have been applied to the Class 47 and later to the Class 56.

We have been able to make an assessment of the relative merits of one large slow-running engine versus two fast-running engines to achieve the same power: when to use one system and when to use the other. In fact, for differing reasons, the alternatives have been perpetuated in the HST and the Class 56, one with two high-speed engines, the other with one large medium-speed. Long after the last locomotive is detached from its last train, the Class 52, the 1000, will be remembered, not only as a faithful workhorse but as a significant development step in railway traction.

Below: When the first 'Western' was under construction drawings were prepared by the BR Design Panel which were coloured in various liveries to be used on the early Class 52 engines. This was a preliminary to deciding on a final standard colour scheme for BR's engines and rolling stock. At that time the 'Westerns' were going to be named after West of England place names and No D1000 was labelled *Cheddar Gorge./Sam Lambert*

Bottom: The last major overhaul of a Class 52 locomotive at Swindon works was when No D1023 was outshopped in 1973. In happier days, when a policy of preventative maintenance rather than repair maintenance was employed, No D1066 *Western Prefect* was nearing completion of an overhaul and repaint at Swindon. */Norman E. Preedy*

Right: The majority of 'Westerns', from Nos D1030 to D1073, were built at Crewe. On 9 September 1962, eleven days before officially entering traffic, No D1040 (later *Western Queen*) received a coat of 'Prestolith' as a protection against body corrosion outside Crewe works.*/John K. Morton*

Bottom right: Only four months after entering traffic in February 1962 No D1001 *Western Pathfinder* (in the maroon livery) was photographed at Swindon, where it was built. The 'Westerns' appeared in several colours including desert sand, maroon, green, golden ochre and blue with a variety of yellow warning panels and front ends. At one stage a competition was held to determine the most popular colour.*/M. Pope*

1X97

WESTERN PATHFINDER
Z 28

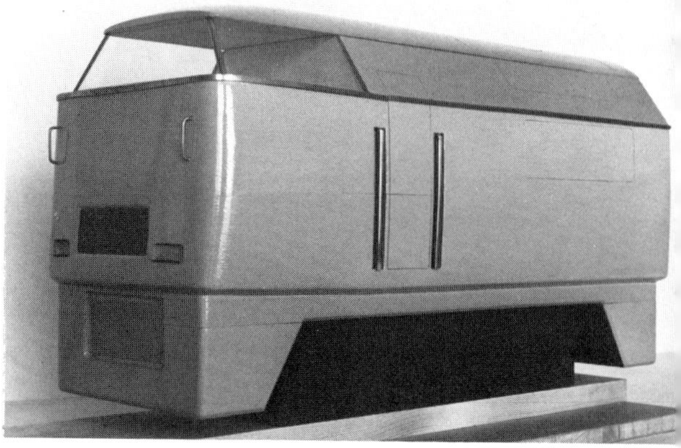

Right: Although the first 'Western' appeared during 1961 plans on basic design were in hand during the late 1950s. By May 1959 the front-end design had been shaped in wood as shown in this official photograph. Although the final design varied considerably, some similarity can be detected, especially in the roofline./*British Rail*

Below: Resplendent in golden ochre with an experimental 'T' yellow warning panel is No D1015 *Western Champion* in the snow at Swindon in January 1963. The shade was compared with a preserved LBSCR 'Terrier' and the paint was subsequently produced at Derby, thus emulating Stroudley's improved engine green of the old London and Brighton!/*Sam Lambert*

Top: An immaculate 'Western', No D1005, descends from the Aynho Junction flyover, on the direct Princes Risborough route, with the 15.10 Paddington to Wolverhampton express on 29 August 1962. Type 4 motive power was required on the Paddington to Birmingham, Wolverhampton and Chester route during the early 1960s as the London Midland line was undergoing electrification; the role was filled by the first 'Westerns' to enter service. */M. Mensing*

Above: This scene is dated by the 'Western' without a yellow warning panel and the 2-6-2 'Prairie' tank engine in the background. No D1006 *Western Stalwart* leaves Princes Risborough with the 07.25 from Wolverhampton to Paddington on 13 September 1962./*H. K. Harman*

Two pictures which reflect 14 years of progress on the Western Region, with the 'Western' diesel-hydraulics replacing steam and in turn being ousted by the High Speed Train with diesel-electric transmission. In the photograph (*Below*) taken on 23 June 1962 No D1005 *Western Venturer* double-heads 'Castle' class 4-6-0 No 5089 *Westminster Abbey* through Barnwood, Gloucester with a Paignton to Wolverhampton working. *Bottom,* D1013 *Western Ranger* paused momentarily beside HST unit No 253 002 at Paddington before working an enthusiasts special to Hereford on 26 September 1976./*Norman Preedy*/*John Vaughan*

Top: Whenever the multiple-unit 'Blue Pullman' sets were unavailable on the prestige 'Birmingham Pullman' a Class 4 (later classified 52) 'Western' diesel-hydraulic and a set of Pullman cars were hastily pressed into service. Such was the case on 12 July 1962 when No D1006 *Western Stalwart*, in maroon livery, was photographed leaving Solihull with the 16.50 down train to Wolverhampton./*M. Mensing*

Above: The original desert sand colour scheme of No D1000 *Western Enterprise* is seen in this picture, taken in July 1962. The locomotive and assortment of Pullman cars and normal coaches were deputising for the usual multiple-unit set as they approached Acock's Green Station with the 13.00 Birmingham Snow Hill to Paddington 'Birmingham Pullman'./*M. Mensing*

IV03

Left: On the approach to Saunderton Tunnel the up and down tracks separate giving the appearance of single lines. On 25 September 1962 No D1005 *Western Venturer* was in charge of the 06.30 from Birkenhead to Paddington./*H. K. Harman*

Above: The British Rail travel centre at Plymouth organised a Western Farewell excursion on 27 November 1976. From Plymouth the train ran via Bristol, Birmingham, Oxford, Basingstoke and Exeter. The engine provided was No 1010 *Western Campaigner*, which is seen here at Oxford, the refuelling stop./*John Vaughan*

Below: No D1037 *Western Empress* was photographed just south of Warwick with IV38, the 12.25 from Birmingham New Street to Paddington, on 14 September 1974. For many years the 'Westerns' were banished from the Birmingham route, but during their first and last three years of service they were regular performers. /*Brian Morrison*

Below: Class 52 *Western Pathfinder* passes the unkempt platforms of Widney Manor in Warwickshire with the 10.25 from Birmingham to London. This former GWR Birmingham route has suffered badly since its reduction to secondary route status, as can be seen by the trackbed on the left of the picture, which once formed part of a four-track main line./*Philip D. Hawkins*

Right: At a time when 'Westerns' were described as 'Type 4, diesel' hydraulic C-C locomotives, No D1049 *Western Monarch* passes stockbroker belt country at Seer Green & Jordans with the 12.10 Paddington to Birkenhead train. This was a time when the GW route to Birkenhead via Birmingham Snow Hill was still in use. The photo was taken on 9 November 1963./*Brian Stephenson*

Bottom right: Having worked a troop train special from Plymouth to Birmingham New Street throughout *Western Glory* was a surprise visitor 'under the wires' at New Street on 19 June 1976. Despite being in poor external condition with the smoky exhausts, No D1072 was still being admired in the rain by a dozen or so trainspotters./*John Vaughan*

1M13

1072
D1072

Above: A panoramic view of the approaches to Paddington. The background has changed considerably in recent years with the construction of new office blocks, the Post Office Tower and the M40 motorway. On 21 May 1975 No D1046 *Western Marquis* heads a down express past Ranelagh Road refuelling depot, where two Class 47s await their next turn of duty./*Brian Morrison*

Right: No D1001 *Western Pathfinder* is seen here speeding through Sonning cutting with a Paddington to Paignton train./*John Vaughan*

Left: Nine air-braked Mark II coaches comprising the 16.05 Paddington to Birmingham passes the silver birches of Sonning cutting behind No 1056 *Western Sultan.* This locomotive was one of five to be fitted with a small air flow ventilator in the cab in an attempt to reduce high temperatures in the summer months. Although the large areas of glass gave the Western crews excellent visibility the cabs did tend to overheat, especially when exposed to direct sunshine./*John Vaughan*

Below: No D1010 *Western Campaigner* accelerates a train of Mark IIB air-braked stock past Waltham St Lawrence in March 1976. This locomotive enjoyed a reputation for fast running, but its speed was reduced to 70mph in the picture below as it crossed from the down fast to the local line with the Sunday 12.30 Paddington to Penzance train on 22 August 1976. The deviation was due to engineering works./*John Vaughan*

Bottom: Western Champion had just completed at least the last part of the journey from Penzance to Paddington on one engine. The time of the year is revealed by the hundreds of flying insects which cover the engine's front end and windscreen. *Western Champion* had the notable distinction of hauling from Handborough to Paddington the Pullman coaches returning from Winston Churchill's funeral./*John Vaughan*

'Westerns' were not an everyday sight on Freightliner trains. However, No D1009 *Western Invader* was captured on film at Ruscombe on 9 March 1976 with a down Freightliner working to South Wales./*John Vaughan*

MASU 490223 7

Above: Assuming that both old and new station clocks were correct and that the departure from Paddington had been at 10.30 sharp, No D1036 *Western Emperor* had taken just 31min to complete the 36mile journey from Paddington to Reading General with a Paignton train on 19 June 1976./*John Vaughan*

Left: A favourite overbridge for WR main line observations is at the entrance to Old Oak Common Diesel Depot and carriage sidings beside the Grand Union Canal. On 27 March 1976 No 1070 *Western Gauntlet* finished its turn and makes for Old Oak Common shed, where it will be refuelled ready for its next working. /*John Vaughan*

Top right: A very clean *Western Ambassador* on the up fast line at Iver, Bucks hauls a mixture of Mark I and Mark II stock including two brake vehicles on the 12.25 Birmingham to Paddington in April 1976. No 1051 was withdrawn in September 1976 when new ballast was inadvertently thrown up into the wiring, causing extensive damage./*John Vaughan*

Right: Just two days before the summer heatwave started *Western Lady* was pressed into service to relieve a failed diesel-electric locomotive on the air-conditioned 14.00 Paignton to Paddington express. The train is seen leaving Reading General on 19 June 1976 almost exactly one hour late. The 'Westerns' were not equipped with Electrical Train Heating (ETH) and they were not able to operate the air conditioning units on the Mark II D/E/F coaches. /*John Vaughan*

00 00

1048

Top right: A roster which was regularly worked by a 'Western' during the early months of 1976 was the 13.15 Paddington to Cardiff train. In this photograph, taken on the 27 April 1976, No D1037 *Western Empress* is shrouded in steam from the steampipe as it waits to leave Paddington./*John Vaughan*

Centre right: Nos D1053 and D1054 at Paddington on 18 September 1976. *Western Patriach* had worked an up overnight train from Plymouth and is seen here at the head of empty stock bound for Old Oak Common. In the background *Western Governor* was in charge of the 08.30 Paddington to Paignton express. If 'Western'-hauled, the 08.30 was a popular train with enthusiasts as the locomotive returned to London with the 15.55 from Paignton, affording 404 miles of Class 52 haulage./*John Vaughan*

Below: From 1 January 1976 the use of train identity headcodes was to be phased out and the indicator blinds of locomotives altered to display 0000. Almost inevitably, within a matter of days, the majority of the 'Westerns' were showing the locomotive number as a headcode, a practice later adopted on the Western Region with Class 50s. Showing the engine number on the headcode blind No D1023 *Western Fusilier* speeds towards Iver with the 14.05 Paddington-Birmingham train./*John Vaughan*

Above: An unusual view of Old Oak Common shed with a pair of 'Westerns' around the turntable. In this view *Western Trooper* is enjoying some late afternoon sun in the company of *Western Prince.* The old steam shed at Old Oak utilised four large turntables, all of which were under cover but only one 'exposed' one survives. The present diesel maintenance depot is geared to major locomotive repairs and assumed an important role when Swindon ceased to handle overhauls and repairs in 1972. The major work on Class 52 locos was, however, executed at Laira diesel depot./*John Vaughan*

Below: A little over 7min after leaving Paddington No D1009 *Western Invader* thunders through West Ealing at the head of the 'Cornish Riviera' on 3 April 1976. The lines diverging on the left of the picture are to Greenford and the former GW Birmingham main line. The down main line platform has been removed leaving only the local platforms for general use. Immediately above the first coach can be seen the milk terminal where the products of Somerset, Devon and Cornwall are pumped into Milk Marketing Board lorries./*John Vaughan*

Top: Right beside the lay-by to the east of Sonning cutting passes the WR main line commanding a fine view of the passing trains. On a sunny April day in 1976, 1071 *Western Renown* races towards Reading with the 14.05 Paddington to Birmingham (New Street) train. When the summer timetable started the balance workings of locomotives rarely resulted in a Class 52 on the Birmingham line, although by the end of the year regular appearances were again being made on LMR territory in the Birmingham area. /*John Vaughan*

Above: Western Champion passes beneath the booking hall of Southall station and slows down to cross from the fast to the up local with a parcels trains. *Champion* was the only 'Western' to appear in golden ochre during 1963, a livery which had LBSCR connections as the colour had been known previously as Stroudley 'improved engine green'./*John Vaughan*

Above: One of the most picturesque parts of the attractive Berks and Hants route to the West is the scenery in and around Somerford. Sweeping through the curves between Somerford and Charlton Mackrell on a glorious spring day is No D1065 *Western Consort* with the 08.35 Penzance to Paddington express./*John Vaughan*

Below: Still clean from use on an enthusiasts' railtour two weeks earlier, No D1009 *Western Invader* lifts the heavy 11.05 Fridays only Penzance to Paddington train past Clink Road signal box on 17 September 1976. The lines to the right of the third coach go to Frome and towards Radstock./*John Vaughan*

1000

1005

Top left: Coming off the Westbury cut-off at 80mph and about to pass Fairwood Junction is the 13.30 Paddington to Penzance express behind No D1071 *Western Renown*. This was another of the locomotives fitted with the cab ventilator (see the small square grille below the windscreen)./*John Vaughan*

Left: With her two Maybach engines at full throttle No D1005 *Western Venturer* finds little trouble in lifting the 13.30 from Paddington to Penzance over Savernake summit. The train is passing the site of Savernake Low Level station, once the junction for Marlborough, which finally closed in 1966./*John Vaughan*

Top: Bedwyn station for the village of Great Bedwyn remains open but is used only by local dmus, plus one commuter train to and from Paddington on Mondays to Fridays. On 20 April 1976 *Western Invader* storms through the station in fine style with a Paignton to Paddington relief carrying passengers who had spent the Easter weekend in the Torbay area./*John Vaughan*

Above: With blossom on the trees and spring in the air No D1028 *Western Hussar* runs down from Savernake past the site of Wolfhall Junction (the connection with the old Midland & South Western Junction Railway) with the 11.00 Plymouth to Paddington on 20 April 1976./*John Vaughan*

Top: Good value for money were the Western Region's Saturday sprees. For only £3 return enthusiasts could often have a cheap day out and enjoy Class 52 motive power. On May Day 1976 No D1028 *Western Hussar* worked such a special from Paddington to Plymouth and was photographed during a crew change at Taunton./*John Vaughan*

Above: During the early 1970s the 'Westerns' had almost a monopoly of the West of England trains. To have a day out along the Kennet and Avon canal in Wiltshire and Berkshire was a joy for the 'Western' enthusiast. There were many points of interest along the line to explore between trains, such as the steam-beam pumping engines at Crofton or Savernake Forest. Heading towards the edge of the forest on 20 April 1976 was No D1071 *Western Renown* on the 12.30 Paddington to Paignton./*John Vaughan*

Right: Seen through one of the long abandoned locks on the disused section of the Kennet and Avon canal between Bedwyn and Crofton is No D1049 *Western Monarch* with the morning Kensington Olympia to St Austell Motorail on 28 June 1975. During 1976 this train was almost exclusively Class 50-hauled, although *Western Patriach* did put in one appearance on 25 September. /*John Vaughan*

Below: A photograph taken from the overbridge abutment where ten years before trains on the old Somerset & Dorset crossed the GWR West of England main line at Cole, near Bruton. No D1001 *Western Pathfinder* is seen at the head of the 11.55 Paignton to Paddington train./*John Vaughan*

Bottom: Class 52 No 1043 *Western Duke* passes Hungerford Common with the up 13.55 from Paignton to Paddington on 28 June 1975. Of special interest is the ex-LNER Gresley buffet car E 9135, the second coach from the engine./*John Vaughan*

Right: A remarkable picture taken at Westbury on 1 April 1976. There seem to be Class 52 locomotives all over the place with No D1071 *Western Renown* at the up platform with the 13.55 Paignton to Paddington and on the right D1013 *Western Ranger* running light to take over a road-stone train, whilst in the centre No D1033 *Western Trooper* prepares to bank a heavy stone train, headed by a Class 47, on to the Southern Region's line down the Wylye Valley to Salisbury./*Philip D. Hawkins*

0000
0000

1B45

Left: The down 'Cornish Riviera Limited' (the 'Rivo') hurries along the South Devon coastline near Dawlish powered by No D1058 *Western Nobleman* on 11 June 1975. The new ballast emphasises the brilliance of the day./*P. J. Fowler*

Bottom left: During the last months of regular express passenger operation the 'Westerns' showed the signs of minimum maintenance, one-engine running being commonplace. The strain of assisting a failed Class 31 earlier in the day must have taken its toll as No D1041 *Western Prince* was itself in trouble at Newton Abbott with the 08.30 London to Paignton train on 11 September 1976. On the left a fitter gazes at the dirt-covered locomotive, whilst the guard (with flag) and driver (with cap) ask another grim-faced fitter whether it will reach Paignton. On the right a member of the station staff walks away in disgust. In the event *Western Prince* reached Paignton, but did not return to London that afternoon as rostered. /*John Vaughan*

Below: It is 09.00 on the sea wall at Dawlish and most holiday-makers are finishing their breakfasts. Just two early risers are on hand to witness *Western Consort* passing on the down road with a mixed freight./*John Vaughan*

Bottom: Aller Junction, Devon, just to the west of Newton Abbott, is where the Torquay and Paignton line leaves the main line to Plymouth. Taking the Plymouth route with the 10.56 Paddington to Penzance summer Saturdays only is No D1036 *Western Emperor*. This locomotive was unique in having its numberplate mounted higher on the cabside than other engines, a fact which is quite obvious in this picture./*John Vaughan*

Top: One of the highlights of the 1976 season came on 11 September when Class 31.416 failed on the down SO Paddington to Barnstaple. After the train had been propelled to Heywood Road Junction by No 1041 *Western Prince* on the 08.30 to Paignton, Westbury provided Class 52 *Western Consort* to haul the defunct 31 and seven coaches to Exeter. On the return journey *Western Consort* was again provided and put in a lively performance with its light load. This was the last through Barnstaple-Paddington train of the 1976 timetable. In this photograph No 1065 is reversing on to its train at the north end of Exeter St Davids, whilst a 'Peak' Class 45 stands in the relief road on spare engine duties./*John Vaughan*

Above: No D1022 *Western Sentinel* leaves Whiteball Tunnel and passes the diminutive Whiteball Siding Signal Box on the 10.56 (SO) from Paddington to Penzance on 15 May 1976. Although this train was advertised as first stop Totnes, the usual practice was to stop on the middle road at Exeter for a crew change./*John Vaughan*

The first of the Class, No D1000 *Western Enterprise*, emerged from Swindon works late in 1961 experimentally painted in desert sand livery, and the then BR crest in raised metal on the cab side. Name and number plates were backed in black.

Above: At first there was indecision between red and green as a livery for the 'Westerns'. After Swindon had turned out the second engine of the class in green livery, it then switched to maroon, by now with a yellow warning 'apron' on the cab ends. The raised metal BR crest was dropped and replaced by the contemporary coaching stock crest on the cab side. Seen here in Sonning cutting, near Reading, at the head of a westbound express is gleaming new No D1010 *Western Campaigner./British Rail*

Top right: Initially the Crewe order for 'Westerns' was finished in an unlined green livery, and red-backed number and nameplate, and again with the BR coaching stock emblem on the cab side. First of the Crewe order, No D1035 *Western Yeoman*, is seen approaching Solihull with the up Saturday 'Cambrian Coast Express' on 25 August 1962./*M. Mensing*

Right: A final livery experiment was conducted on No D1015 *Western Champion*, which was turned out and ran for a period in golden ochre livery. Note also the experimental turning back of the yellow warning 'apron' into a short line along the cab side leading to the BR crest./*British Rail*

1A70

D 1015
WESTERN CHAMPION

Eventually maroon became the standard livery of the class until the advent of BR blue. This picture shows one of the final deliveries, No D1071 *Western Renown*, pausing at Reading with an up express from the West. A Hymek diesel-hydraulic is overtaking on the up through line./*British Rail*

51
1A26

Above: When the BR blue livery was first applied the yellow warning 'apron' was still in vogue, as seen on this picture of No D1037 *Western Empress* waiting to leave Plymouth with the London-bound 'Cornish Riviera Express'./*British Rail*

Right: The final appearance of the 'Westerns', with the full yellow warning panel on the cab ends: No D1069 *Western Vanguard* heads a stone train from Merehead quarry towards Witham on 6 July 1971./*Ivo Peters*

6Z00

Another view of the final 'Western' class livery: No D1057 *Western Chieftain* takes a Plymouth-Paddington express through Dawlish on 12 June 1974./*Derek Cross*

Above: Powering through Totnes on a hot June day in 1969 is No D1030 *Western Musketeer* on the down 'Cornishman' from Bradford Exchange to Plymouth and Penzance. The 'Cornishman' eventually lost its named status after the 1974/75 timetable and became just another cross-country train from the North to the West Country./*L. Riley*

Below: Evening at Mutley tunnel in July 1976. At precisely twenty minutes to eight o'clock, an oil-covered and grimy *Western Prince* emerges from the tunnel (now disguised as a car park) and passes two interesting poster advertisements which suggest that photographing 'Westerns' was not the only pleasure of 1976. The down parcels train terminated at Plymouth and No D1041 returned to Laira for servicing./*John Vaughan*

10

Left: Having completed the journey with the 08.30 from Paddington No D1054 *Western Governor* pulls the empty stock out of Paignton Station for Goodrington Sidings. The track and semaphore signal on the right of the picture belong to the Torbay and Dartmouth Railway. There are moves afoot to preserve a 'Western' for use on this stretch of line as an alternative to the usual steam locomotives./*John Vaughan*

Above: In the early evening of 23 July 1976 No D1009 *Western Invader* leaves a dense trail of exhaust fumes over Plymouth as it departs with a parcels/perishables train bound for London. /*John Vaughan*

Right: Storming the formidable Daignton bank at Stoneycombe Quarries on the 22 May 1976 is No D1065 *Western Consort* with the summer Saturdays only 09.50 through train from Paddington to Newquay. Just above the cab of the 'Western' can be seen the last coach of an up train and this gives some indication of the curvature of the line./*John Vaughan*

Right: One of the most popular galleries in the country for train watching must be the sea wall between Exminster and Teignmouth. Holiday crowds over the decades have waved to passing trains whether hauled by 'Kings', 'Castles' or Westerns'. The only sad thing about this scene is that the small boy being held on the wall by his father will not be seeing 'Westerns' on his next holiday by the seaside. On 23 July 1976, an overcast day in a largely cloudless summer, No D1072 *Western Glory* heads the 12-bogie 07.30 Paddington to Penzance, a train which included two luggage vehicles and two buffet cars!/*John Vaughan*

Below: Towards the end of their days some of the 'Westerns' were looking delapidated due to the effects of weathering and the harsh treatment from chemicals in the water used in carriage washing plants. The poor condition of *Western Champion's* paintwork is evident in this picture as she accelerates the 10.56 SO Paddington to Penzance away from Totnes on 31 July 1976./*John Vaughan*

Above: A long haul of covered china clay wagons accelerate away from Lostwithiel behind No D1023 *Western Fusilier*. The empties have been brought up from Carne Point on the Fowey branch and after reversal are being hauled to St Blazey. The photograph was taken from Lostwithiel goods shed./*John Vaughan*

Below: An immaculate *Western Patriarch*, gleaming after a Laira repaint, leaves Liskeard exactly on time with five coaches of the down 'Cornish Riviera Limited' on 4 July 1975. The letter 'D' on the cast numberplate has been painted out. Whilst this conformed with the elimination nationally of the 'D' prefix, the 'Westerns' never did succumb to class numbering./*John Vaughan*

Top: **Starting out on the 305mile journey to London is the 12.20** from Penzance. The six air-braked coaches will be increased to 10 or 11 at Plymouth, where a restaurant car and other vehicles are added. No D1065 *Western Consort* is travelling up on what used to be exclusively the down line. This stretch of track is now treated as a single line and used by trains in both directions. The other tracks in the picture are used for empty stock movements and storage. The Royal Mail stock behind the locomotive is used on the up 'Night Postal' to London./*John Vaughan*

Above: Subject of controversy was the demolition of the Brunel-designed station building on the down side of Lostwithiel station. The action of local pressure groups prevented the up building **suffering a similar fate when the Department of the Environment** issued a preservation order. The awning of the down building had just been demolished when *Western Champion* passed on the 11.38 Penzance to Leeds on Sunday 16 May 1976./*John Vaughan*

Right: A splendid sight on a super day is No D1015 *Western Champion* complying with the 15mph limit as it passes from Cornwall into Devon and leaves the Royal Albert Bridge. The photo was taken from a small park which provides a panoramic view of both road and rail bridges, Saltash and the River Tamar. The train is the 10.20 Penzance to Birmingham./*John Vaughan*

I.K.BRUNEL
ENGINEER
1859
1015

Above: No D1054 *Western Governor* lifts the 10.20 Penzance to Birmingham past Burngullow signalbox and towards St Austell on 19 May 1976. The branch on the right to Drinnick Mill once continued through the heart of China clay country to St Dennis Junction on the Newquay line. Burngullow station closed in 1931./*John Vaughan*

Left: One of the staple commodities to be transported from Cornwall by rail is milk. Once per day, some time after 16.00 hours, the up milk train for Ealing and Kensington in the London area leaves St Erth. Framed by a rather interesting loading gauge at St Erth is No D1009 *Western Invader*. The locomotive will pick up further milk tank wagons at Lostwithiel and arrive in London in the small hours of the morning./*John Vaughan*

Left: A view from the end of the GWR main line at Penzance, so long a stronghold of the 'Westerns'. On a perfect day the visibility towards Marazion and St Michaels Mount is excellent. In the foreground *Western Governor* stands silent with engines switched off until departure later in the afternoon. Note the neat flower arrangement around the Penzance nameboard./*John Vaughan*

Below: A before-breakfast photograph in the most attractive part of the Fowey Valley. Through the woods to the east of Bodmin Road No D1051 *Western Ambassador* gets to grip with 07.40 Penzance to Liverpool train and picks up speed across Pendalake Viaduct. /*John Vaughan*

Top: Past the rooftops of Plymouth and on to the viaduct to the west of North Road station is *Western Gauntlet* with the Penzance to Plymouth portion of the 14.30 to London. The fourth coach is on the site of the West Junction, where the line to Plymouth Millbay once crossed the disused bridge supports on the left of the picture. /*John Vaughan*

Above: Growling up the steep hill towards Doublebois is *Western Ambassador* with a very heavy train of tanker wagons containing china clay slurry. The load will be discharged at a paper mill in North Kent./*John Vaughan*

Top right: In torrential rain No D1005 *Western Venturer* shows a trace of exhaust as she eases the up perishables containing flowers and market garden produce past the Truro starter signal. Truro is the junction for Falmouth and on Summer Saturdays a 'Western' could occasionally be seen on the branch with the 09.10 through train from Falmouth to Paddington./*John Vaughan*

Right: Having received the 'right away' the driver of No D1054 *Western Governor* leans out of his cab at Par to see the cause of delay to the 16.10 Penzance to Paddington train. One of the problems of train operation in Cornwall in the summer months is the loading of luggage and for the need at some stations to 'pull up' a long train, thus making two stops necessary at one station./*John Vaughan*

1005

D 1054
WESTERN GOVERNOR

Above: Set in the valley of the River Fowey about four miles from Bodmin is Bodmin Road station. The occasional bus service now provides the connection for Bodmin and Padstow, whereas until 1967 the branch train would be waiting at the island platform. The branch to Wenford Bridge and Wadebridge still sees some traffic hauled by either a Class 08 shunter or a Class 25. No D1026 *Western Centurion* is seen on the main line with an up express in 1975./*John Vaughan*

Right: The 13.55 Penzance to Birmingham train headed by No D1071 *Western Renown* approaches Wearde Quay near the site of Defiance Platform (closed in October 1930) on 20 May 1976. /*John Vaughan*

Top: 11.40 at Par in Cornwall during the long dry summer of 1976. No D1058 *Western Nobleman* is about to enter the station with a Newquay train. The locomotive was just over halfway through a very demanding 24 hours. It had worked the 23.45 Paddington to Penzance throughout, the Penzance to Par ECS (empties), the 11.41 Par to Newquay, 13.23 Newquay to Plymouth and the 16.40 Plymouth to Paddington, pausing only for fuel at Penzance — sterling work for a locomotive in less than peak condition. */John Vaughan*

Above: Struggling up the Fowey Valley from Bodmin Road to Liskeard No D1036 *Western Emperor* crosses Clinnick Viaduct with an up parcels/perishables train from Penzance. On this day the load contained a Mark II TSO coach and a Mark I BSK, resembling a mixed train on some remote light railway. */John Vaughan*

Top: An interesting assortment of freight vehicles from St Blazey is seen crossing Moorswater Viaduct near Liskeard behind No D1065 *Western Consort* on the evening of 17 May 1976. Between the bridge arches can be seen the piers of Brunel's original structure. /*John Vaughan*

Above: One of the most fascinating phenomena of the Cornish countryside is the abundance of derelict mines with their tall gaunt engine houses often covered in ivy. This fine example at Scorrier to the east of Redruth is passed by No D1056 *Western Sultan* setting a brisk pace with the 09.30 from Paddington to Penzance. /*John Vaughan*

Above: Passing along the edge of the estuary of the River Tywi near Ferryside station with the 08.26 SO Paddington to Fishguard is No D1025 *Western Guardsman* on 3 August 1974. The leading vehicle is of LNER origin./*A. W. Hobson*

Below: Two members of the class had rotary windscreen wiper systems fitted as an experiment. However the large metal mounting ring and wiper arm distracted the driver and reduced visibility. At the head of a 12-coach 'Capitals United Express' D1039 *Western King* is near Rumney River Bridge Junction on 19 May 1964. Nos D1039 and D1006 were refitted with conventional windscreens in due course and the experiment, other than on exceptionally wet days, was deemed to be a failure./*S. Rickard*

Having arrived from the harbour of Fishguard No D1068 *Western Reliance* trundles away from Swansea High Street station for Landore motive power depot and refuelling on 17 July 1976.
/John Vaughan

1O68

Passenger Terminal

Top left: This photograph of *Western Pathfinder* was taken from the 08.25 Paddington to Fishguard whilst travelling at 40mph through Newport station on 21 August 1976. No D1001 passes an inspection saloon in the sidings with an up parcels train. */John Vaughan*

Left: Despite a suggestion that Class 52 locomotives would not be seen west of Swansea after 1975 the summer Saturday 07.53 and, more likely, 08.25 trains from Paddington to Fishguard regularly produced a 'Western' in 1976. On a superb day in July 1976 D1068 *Western Reliance* provided the motive power for the 08.25 departure. The roster then provided for the locomotive and stock to form the 14.30 from Fishguard to Swansea. No D1068 waits to depart whilst the crowds on the deck of the MV *Avalon* wait for the ship's departure to Rosslare in Southern Ireland.*/John Vaughan*

Above: In maroon livery and with only a few months in service No D1016 *Western Gladiator* was photographed approaching Neath with a Paddington to Swansea express on 27 August 1963.*/D. J. Wall*

Top: In South Wales with two class 37 engines as stablemates No D1070 *Western Gauntlet* ticks over on the reception road at Cardiff Canton after coming off the 07.53 Paddington to Fishguard on 14 August 1976. The locomotive had a suspected flat tyre and was due for examination later in the afternoon./*John Vaughan*

Above: The last Class 52 working of the 1976 Fishguard boat trains was on 4 September when Old Oak Common provided No 1041 *Western Prince* as motive power. *Prince* worked through to Fishguard, whereas one or two Christmas boat trains were 'Western'-hauled but to Swansea only. This photograph shows 1041 at Neath./*John Vaughan*

Above: The other Gloucester station is Central, which has been modernised since this picture was taken. On 11 June 1969 No D1057 *Western Chieftain* heads a load of steel block from South Wales./*Norman E. Preedy*

Below: The IV86 from Bradford to Paignton, headed by No D1041 *Western Prince*, leaves Gloucester Eastgate and passes Midland Road crossing on 4 August 1970. The 'Western' has just relieved the 'Peak' class locomotive seen on the left of the picture. This was the former Midland Railway line from Birmingham to Bristol and under a rationalisation scheme announced in 1975 Eastgate was closed, all of the track seen in this picture ripped up and traffic diverted to the former GW Gloucester Central station. This necessitates the reversal of many passenger trains./*Norman E. Preedy*

BLAKEDOWN
6V53

Top left: A rare picture of the 04.27 Stoke to St Blazey 'Clayliner' empties at Blakedown (once known as Churchill & Blakedown) on 17 February 1974 hauled by No D1021 *Western Cavalier*. 'Clayliner' trains were diverted over part of the old Oxford & Wolverhampton Railway between Norton Junction and Dudley, thence to Bescot, from 1 October 1973, thus bringing regular diesel-hydraulic workings into the heart of the Black Country./*Geoffrey Bannister*

Left: Photographs of 'Westerns' between Gloucester and Severn Tunnel Junction are unusual, but the camera captured this shot of No D1026 *Western Centurion* between Newnham and Lydney on the 08.00 Reading to Severn Tunnel (via Gloucester) freight. A glimpse of the River Severn can be seen through the arch of the overbridge./*B. J. Ashworth*

Top: One does not normally associate 'Westerns' with the 'Cambrian Coast Express', but in the early 1960s the class regularly worked north-west of Birmingham to Shrewsbury and Chester. A maroon-coloured No D1020 *Western Hero* at the head of a set of maroon coaches passes the vast mechanical signalbox and into Shrewsbury station with the down working on 24 August 1963. /*Ian G. Holt*

Above: At the head of a British Rail special from Paddington to the steam open day at Bulmers, Hereford depot on 26 September was No D1013 *Western Ranger*. The train had reversed at Newport on the outward journey and is seen here entering Hereford for the return journey via Worcester Foregate Street, the Lickey Incline and Birmingham New Street./*John Vaughan*

Below: In October 1963 a maroon 'Western' with small yellow warning panel, No D1054 *Western Governor*, leaves Sapperton Tunnel and passes Frampton Mansell Village on the Swindon to Gloucester route with an Acton to Cardiff goods train. In days of steam heavy coal trains from South Wales used this route to avoid congestion on the main line between Swindon and Severn Tunnel Junction. Sadly parts of the route have been reduced to single track and the main traffic comprises a three-car dmu running a shuttle service between Cheltenham, Gloucester and Swindon. 'Westerns' never were a particularly common sight on the Sapperton route. /*Norman E. Preedy*

Bottom: During the last two weeks of the 1976 summer timetable many of the 'Westerns' had their steam-heating pipes refitted, which enabled them to reappear on the overnight trains to the West Country. This meant that the 11.15 from Paddington to Cardiff, which utilises one of the overnight locomotives, was frequently 'Western'-hauled. The engine and stock return from Cardiff as the 15.25 to Paddington via Gloucester. This meant not only a journey past Chepstow but the opportunity of experiencing a 'Western' assault of Sapperton. On September 25 No D1013 *Western Ranger* was produced for the round trip and is seen here at Stroud in the Cotswold hills, as 'Peak' No 46.023, descends from Sapperton with a lightweight goods./*John Vaughan*

Top: The scene is Didcot on 12 May 1976. *Western Sultan* is in charge of the 13.15 Paddington to Cardiff train, which with only a seven-coach load spent 9min at the station waiting for time. In the background can be seen the massive cooling towers of Didcot power station and the remains of the Old Storage House in the provender yard which was being demolished./*John Vaughan*

Above: A rare photograph of No D1041 *Western Prince* passing Hawkeridge Junction, just outside Westbury, with the Royal Train conveying Her Majesty the Queen to the West Country for an official visit on 3 June 1966./*Ivo Peters*

Below: Crewe-built 'Westerns' up and down at Swindon. In May 1972 No D1038 *Western Sovereign* waits to depart for Paddington from Swindon's island platform, whilst No D1070 *Western Gauntlet* is passing at speed on the down through road with a Bristol express./*Norman E. Preedy*

Bottom: A nicely framed picture of a 'Western' in maroon livery with a small yellow warning panel. On a clear March day in 1968 No D1027 *Western Lancer* leaves Bristol and passes Bedminster Park with the empty stock of a London to Bristol train. The old GW-type lower-quadrant semaphore signals were replaced in the Bristol area in 1971./*David Wharton*

Right: Having passed Pilning an unidentified Class 52 locomotive races towards the darkness of the Severn Tunnel with the 14.00 Paddington to Swansea train on 7 August 1972, before air-conditioned coaches were introduced on this route. Their introduction drastically reduced the number of 'Western' workings into South Wales./*John Cooper-Smith*

1C63

T
1C27

1M91

Top left: Having passed through the Severn Tunnel No D1060 *Western Dominion* has just finished applying the air brakes as the 10.00 Paddington to Swansea train enters a permanent way slack at Magor on the way to Newport on 30 May 1972./*Geoff Gillham*

Left: With the vast overall roof of Bristol Temple Meads station behind, an immaculate *Western Talisman*, having taken on water, waits for the right-away at the front of the 07.55 from Plymouth to Liverpool Lime Street on 24 February 1968. D1007 eventually came to grief near West Ealing when one of the battery box covers became unfastened and struck a points control box. The train was derailed, the locomotive ended up on its side and several passengers were killed./*P. J. Fowler*

Above: Looking spick and span in the unusual livery of BR blue with a small yellow warning panel is No D1057 *Western Chieftain* at Bath Spa, that fine city with majestic Georgian terraces and elegant iron railings. The train is the 11.15 Bristol to Paddington and the date 9 March 1968./*David Wharton*

3A45

Left: Another occasional Class 52 working in the early 1970s was the 09.00 Saturdays only from Paddington to Tenby, on the Pembroke Dock Branch in South West Wales. No D1030 *Western Musketeer* nears the end of its 250mile run from the capital and passes through dense woodland near the site of the closed Templeton station. The train's headcode suggests that this is an up and not a down train./*K. C. Taylor*

Above: In addition to branch lines with passenger services there are several mineral and freight only lines which see 2,700hp locomotive workings from time to time. On the old Lostwithiel to Fowey branch 'Westerns' worked the heavier china clay trains from Burngullow and St Blazey to Carne Point, loading there on to ships for export. *Western Fusilier* is seen crossing a short causeway at the secluded Golant harbour, where the only intermediate station on the branch was situated, and which closed to passengers in 1965. /*John Vaughan*

One of the delights of a summer Saturday is the sight of through loco-hauled trains from London or the Midlands on to some of the minor branch lines, especially those serving seaside resorts. These two pictures (*right and next page*) show No D1058 *Western Nobleman* on the Newquay branch in Cornwall. (*Right*) This photograph was taken from the leading coach as No D1058 pounded up the meandering single line in the picturesque Luxulyan Valley with a 12-coach load on 6 August 1976. (*Next page)* having arrived at Newquay *Nobleman* is seen running round its train in readiness for its departure with the 13.23 through train to Paddington./*John Vaughan*

Way out

1058
ROOMS

Below: A summer Saturday working which often produced a 'Western' in 1976 was the Derby to Weymouth through train which, after changing engines, left Bristol Temple Meads at 09.38. On 12 June 1976 Bath Road depot supplied No D1005 *Western Venturer* for the working, which is seen here at Weymouth station. /*Norman E. Preedy*

Bottom: An uncommon photograph of a 'Western' on an up fitted freight between Yeovil Junction and Yeovil Pen Mill stations. The passenger service between the former Southern and Western Region lines ceased in 1968 and the line from Pen Mill to Yeovil Town (the track bed of which can be seen in the foreground) closed to passengers in November 1965. *Western Ranger* was working towards Westbury on the Friday before the Spring Bank holiday weekend in 1976./*John Vaughan*

Right: A glimpse of *Western Sultan's* cab from a Southern Region three-coach 'tadpole' dmu at Reading./*John Vaughan*

D 1056

Left: No D1065 *Western Consort* was ticking-over at Exeter Riverside depot when photographed from the shadows of St Davids station in September 1976./*John Vaughan*

Below: With droplets of rain forming on the window of Truro signalbox a vision of an up 'Western' can be detected. The locomotive is in fact No D1005 *Western Venturer* on the up Penzance perishables./*John Vaughan*

Right: Seen through the trees to the west of Hayle viaduct is No D1049 *Western Monarch* with the 09.20 Liverpool to Penzance on 1 July 1974./*Philip D. Hawkins*

Top: **A regular twice weekly working throughout 1976 was the** Westbury to Leagrave (North of Luton) stone train. The stone from Somerset quarries was worked throughout by the Western Region locomotive, which was often a Class 52 diesel-hydraulic. Such was the case on 21 September, when No D1022 *Western Sentinel* was photographed passing Harpenden, on the ex-Midland Railway, returning to Westbury with empty wagons./*John Vaughan*

Above: The line to Merehead leaves the West Country main line at Witham. Until October 1966 Witham boasted a passenger station and indeed before September 1963 was the junction for Shepton Mallet and all stations to Yatton. Now a signalbox is the only railway building at the junction, and from it this photograph was taken. No D1001 *Western Pathfinder* cautiously descends from Merehead with 38 loaded wagons./*John Vaughan*

Top right: **With the stately spire of Salisbury Cathedral in the** background No D1051 *Western Ambassador* makes for the Wylye Valley with Basingstoke to Westbury stone empties on 9 August 1976. 'Western'-hauled stone trains were frequent visitors to Salisbury and on to the Southern Region, not only to Basingstoke, but to Botley and Fareham./*Geoff Gillham*

Right: A lengthy stone train descends from the summit at Savernake and clings to Crofton curve on 20 April 1976 behind No D1065 *Western Consort*./*John Vaughan*

1051

1065

Above: The London to Lostwithiel and St Erth milk empties leave Acton at about 19.15, but it is 03.17 by the time they leave Plymouth. This picture shows a typical Unigate Creameries six-wheel tank wagon holding 3,000 gallons of milk. *Western Consort* heads the train, which is waiting for the right away from North Road on 24 July 1976./*John Vaughan*

Centre right: Plymouth North Road on the morning of 24 July 1976, almost four months to the day before No D1054 *Western Governor* was withdrawn from service. She was one of the last dozen 'Westerns' to survive. The locomotive was seen frequently west of Plymouth in 1976 and in the photograph was waiting to disappear into the darkness with the 02.50 to Penzance./*John Vaughan*

Bottom right: A night study of the front end of a class 52. No D1022 *Western Sentinel* was photographed in the middle of the night at Plymouth with a down mail train./*John Vaughan*

Above: A delightful photograph of No D1064 *Western Regent* in afternoon sun passing through the rolling hills near Charfield, Gloucestershire. The train is the 09.20 Bradford to Bristol and the date is 5 April 1970. During the late 1960s and early 1970s it was common to find coaches of both maroon and grey/blue livery in one train, especially on the inter-Regional workings. The first coach in this picture is maroon and carries the old BR emblem. /*P. J. Fowler*

Below: In cold and wintry surroundings at Somerton No D1037 *Western Empress* hurries the 08.30 from Paddington down to Paignton on 26 February 1973./*P. J. Fowler*

Above: A telephoto lens is used to effect in this picture of the 'Cornish Riviera Limited' sweeping through the cuttings and curves to the east of Somerton, headed by No D1064 *Western Regent* in 1973./*P. J. Fowler*

Below: A fine spectacle through the gate to the towpath of the Kennet and Avon canal is the 12-coach, 12.30 London to Paignton train, powered by Class 52 No D1049 *Western Monarch* on 16 June 1973. The photograph was taken between Great Bedwyn and Crofton in Wiltshire./*P. J. Fowler*

Top: After Class 47 No 47.108 had run out of fuel on the 11.10 Penzance to Manchester No D1022 *Western Sentinel* was summoned to provide assistance. The defunct Brush and train is seen here, 'Western'-hauled, passing Yatton station exactly one hour late on 21 August 1976. To the right of the photograph the old Clevedon branch once diverged./*John Vaughan*

Above: A rare combination captured in this July 1970 photograph near Dawlish Warren was Class 52 No 1057 *Western Chieftain* double-heading the IM 23 Paignton to Manchester train with Class 45 'Peak' No 117. No 1057 is in the unusual livery of BR blue with a small yellow warning panel./*Norman E. Preedy*

Cornwall is renowned for its bridges and viaducts and these are two of the more impressive ones. (*Below*) No D1010 *Western Campaigner* gives assistance to an English Electric Class 50 on the 08.35 Penzance to Paddington express, which is seen crossing St Pinnock Viaduct, the highest in Cornwall. (*Bottom*) A Class 52 double-heads a Class 47 on Coldrennick Viaduct near Menheniot with the down 'Cornish Riviera' on 2 September 1973./*John Vaughan/John Cooper-Smith*

Above: Super-power was provided for the two coaches and two vans of the 18.00 Penzance to Bristol train on 15 May 1976 in the shape of Class 52s Nos D1022 *Western Sentinel* and D1013 *Western Ranger*. Here they make light work of the climb past Mount in the Fowey Valley between Bodmin Road and Doublebois.
/*John Vaughan*

Below: Western Marquis and *Western Musketeer* join forces in providing ample motive power for the Sunday 10.30 Paddington-Penzance on 17 August 1975 at St Austell. The 'Westerns' were not equipped for multiple working and it was necessary to have a crew in each locomotive when double-heading was employed.
/*Norman E. Preedy*

Below: Double-heading with Class 52s was rare, except in Cornwall, when at one time this was a daily occurrence for operational reasons. However, on 9 March 1968 the photographer captured on film the 11.50 Plymouth to Manchester, double-headed by two maroon 'Westerns' Nos D1028 *Western Hussar* and D1025 *Western Guardsman*, as they passed Bedminster near Bristol. /*David Wharton*

Bottom: 'Western' action at Penzance as 5,400hp of Maybach power is unleashed on the 14.40 to Paddington, headed by Nos D1059 *Western Empire* and D1008 *Western Harrier*. In the foreground a third 'Western', No D1048 *Western Lady*, marshalls a parcels train on 29 August 1973./*Philip D. Hawkins*

Above: A photograph taken in the cab of a 'Western' showing the driver at his controls. The power has been shut off and the instruments reveal that the engines were idling at 650rpm, and the train was travelling at 44mph. The driver's left hand is on the vacuum brake, the adjacent taller handle being the air brake control. Of special interest are the tools of trade; sheet of paper with notations of train timings; tea cup; and tobacco tin. The 'Westerns' rode well at all speeds except 60mph, when the crew would experience a pronounced vertical 'bounce'. At higher speeds the 'Westerns' ran very smoothly indeed./*John Vaughan*

Right: How a 'Western' should look. Specially painted by apprentices at BR Engineering Ltd Swindon for their Open Day was No D1062 *Western Courier* (then withdrawn from service). After standing on exhibit for all to see from the nearby main line, the locomotive was subsequently purchased by the 'Western Locomotive Association' for preservation and eventual use on the Torbay and Dartmouth Railway's line from Paignton to Kingswear./*John Vaughan*

0000

A regular off-Region journey for 'Westerns' was on the 10.55 Acton to Norwood freight. The locomotive provided had normally worked an up overnight train from Plymouth earlier in the day and it is not therefore surprising that a Laira Class 52 often found itself in Norwood Yard. No 1021 *Western Cavalier* was photographed passing Kensington Olympia on the West London Line, returning to the Western Region on 24 March 1976./*Brian Morrison*

Top: A rare visit of a Class 52 to Derby occurred on 29 March 1975, when a PRS/WRC Railtour visited the City. The locomotive used was No D1052 *Western Viceroy*, seen here running round the train at Derby. The locomotive employed a unique system of cab ventilation, quite different from the five sister engines with control panel vents. The ventilators for the system adopted for No D1052 can be seen at the top lip of the bodywork above the windscreens. */Norman E. Preedy*

The following photographs show just a sample of the 'Western' enthusiast specials during 1976/77. On 30 October 1976 a double-headed excursion called 'Westerns South Western' (*Above*) travelled from Paddington to Meldon Quarry behind D1009 *Western Invader* and No D1023 *Western Fusilier*, seen here at Exeter St Davids. On 20 November the Western Locomotive Association ran a unique tour from Kings Cross to York with No D1023. (*Top right*) This photo shows the 'Western Talisman' just after arrival at York. */John Vaughan*

Right: On 4 December the author organised an overnight trip to Cornwall to visit three Cornish branch lines. The photograph shows No D1023 *Western Fusilier* waiting to depart from Paddington at 00.30.*/John Vaughan*

THE

WESTERN
CHINA CLAY

Below: D1056 *Western Sultan* during a photographic stop at Bugle on the Newquay branch. The train was called the 'Western China Clay'./*John Vaughan*

Bottom: On 29 January 1977 the 'Western Memorial' railtour ran from Paddington to Swindon and Crewe thereby visiting the two birthplaces of the 'Westerns' in the same day. This photograph shows No 1023 *Western Fusilier* waiting to depart for Chester whilst in the foreground Class 86/2 No 86.250 glides quietly to a halt and makes a strange but interesting comparison with its hydraulic invader./*John Vaughan*

Above: The first and last time a 'Western' visited the Rhondda Valley was on the 'Western Requiem' Relief train on Sunday 13 February 1977. This view of typical Welsh Valley scenery shows No 1010 *Western Campaigner* pulling out of Treherbert. This trip was so popular that specials with identical itineraries were run on consecutive Sundays./*John Vaughan*

Right: The last 'Western'-hauled train to leave Paddington for the West via the Berks and Hants was No 1048 *Western Lady* on the 'Western Lament' private train hired from BR Western Region by the author on 24 February 1977. The locomotive had the distinction of being the sole surviving Crewe built 'Western' to remain in service and although *Lady* acted as spare on BRs 'Western Tribute' this was to be her last journey at the head of a train. The special ran to Castle Cary and Frome, and is seen here backing on to its train having run round at Castle Cary./*John Vaughan*

Above: The very end came on 26 February 1977 when BR ran the 'Western Tribute' special. The train was double-headed throughout by Nos 1013 *Western Ranger* and 1023 *Western Fusilier*. The route was Paddington-Swansea-Plymouth-Paddington. The fine spectacle of two Class 52s is seen here crossing the viaduct on the approach to Llandore curve, Swansea on the outward journey./*John Vaughan*

Right: The headboard having been raffled earlier in the day it was left to the members of the Western Locomotive Association to apply a fitting 'The End' sticker to No 1023 before returning to London, whilst a personal tribute by a group of regular 'Western' followers in the form of a floral wreath added to the occasion. The return journey was tinged with sadness and there were many enthusiasts in tears as the Maybach engines gave their best on the last climb to Hemerdon summit. There was an atmosphere of disbelief at Paddington when it was suddenly realised that this really was the end of the 'Westerns' on BR. A most distinctive class had passed on leaving a gaping hole in the ranks of the non standard. To many the last throw of Swindon and the GWR had finished and only the scrap yard remained. The train is seen here at Plymouth North Road. /*John Vaughan*

Top right: Face to face in the Swindon graveyard these 'Westerns', stripped of their engines and any reusable parts, stand silent and forlorn. It is sad to reflect that never again will they storm out of Paddington, receive the waves of the crowd along the sea wall at Teignmouth or cross the Tamar into Cornwall./*John Vaughan*

Centre right: Dozens of Maybach MD 655 engines removed from scrapped 'Westerns' create an almost bizarre pattern at Swindon scrap yard./*John Vaughan*

Below: The last journey for three withdrawn 'Westerns' from Laira to Swindon. *Western Queen*, *Western Lord* and *Western Marquis* take a breather in Taunton yard on May Day 1976 before continuing their melancholy journey to the scrap yard. /*John Vaughan*

At the other end of the yard was a sad reminder of the fate suffered by the majority of 'Westerns', the scrap line. Looking very sorry for itself and bearing a suitable inscription *Western Stalwart* awaits the breakers' torch in May 1976./*John Vaughan*